## Susie Ghahremani

# BALANCE
# the BIRDS

Abrams Appleseed
New York

Here come
the birds!

# Half on the left side,

# and half on the right.

# This is how

# the birds balance!

# Uh-oh! Off they go!

# Half the birds remain.

# One side is too heavy.

# One side is too light.

Unless . . .

. . . two
perch
here,

and
two hop
there . . .

# Now the birds balance!

One small
bird remains.

Until . . .

Small birds are
quite light,

but a few more might . . .

BALANCE!

# Here come the birds!

# How will you

# balance the birds?

# For Lilly, who keeps me balanced

Thank you to my flock: Michael, my family,
Stefanie, Traci, Alyssa, Abrams, BuyOlympia, Caitlin,
Gerry, SCBWI, and you, little reader. xo sg

The illustrations in this book were painted
in gouache and colored digitally.

Cataloging-in-Publication Data has been applied for
and may be obtained from the Library of Congress.

ISBN 978-1-4197-2876-1

Text and illustration copyright © 2018 Susie Ghahremani / boygirlparty.com.
Book design by Alyssa Nassner

Printed and bound in China
10 9 8 7 6 5 4 3

For bulk discount inquiries, contact
specialsales@abramsbooks.com.

**ABRAMS** The Art of Books
195 Broadway, New York, NY 10007
abramsbooks.com